COASTLINES
OF AMERICA

COASTLINES
OF AMERICA

J.A. KRAULIS   RON WATTS

GALLERY BOOKS
an imprint of W.H. Smith Publishers, Inc.,
112 Madison Avenue
New York, New York 10016

PAGE ONE:

The cool blue of surging water contrasts the warmth of the sun's setting rays at Montana De Oro State Park.

PAGE TWO:

Kalalau Beach, Kauai in the Hawaiian Islands, bathed in eerie morning glow.

PAGE THREE:

In Gros Morne National Park, Newfoundland, tremendous cliffs imprison Western Brook Pond, which nearly reaches the sea.

PAGE FIVE:

Pools and wet sand at low tide reflect the fading light at dusk in Samuel H. Boardman State Park, Oregon.

Copyright © 1990 by J.A. Kraulis.

Published in Canada by Discovery Books

First published in the United States in 1991 by Gallery Books, an imprint of W.H. Smith Publishers Inc., 112 Madison Avenue, New York, New York 10016

ISBN 0-8317-1488-3

Gallery Books are available for bulk purchase for sales promotions and premium use. For details write or telephone the Manager of Special Sales, W.H. Smith Publishers, Inc., 112 Madison Avenue, New York, New York 10016 (212) 532-6600

Typesetting: Computer Composition of Cda., Inc.
Printed and bound in Hong Kong

C O N T E N T S

INTRODUCTION

THE ONLY LINES ON ORDINARY MAPS THAT HAVE A DIRECT correspondence with nature are water lines: the shores of lakes, the courses of rivers and, above all, the coasts of continents. Lines of latitude, longitude and those denoting contour are lines that do not appear in the actual world. Political boundaries, though they may also sometimes mark the land itself, denote paper claims and agreements. Roads, railways and city blocks, while physical enough, are still man-made additions to the primeval geography. But the coast of a continent is a unique line, potent on maps, in reality and in our imagination.

When the first photographs of earth came back from space, they had very little in common with maps. Clouds obscured parts of the picture, nations were indistinguishable, colors were completely different, highways and even cities were virtually invisible. And yet, these new and unprecedented views of our planet were instantly recognizable. They shared one thing in common with our familiar maps: the shapes of the continents

Montana De Oro State Park, California. Viewed from a bluff high above, a wave fans out across a beach in a secluded cove.

delineated by water lines. More than we are aware, our sense of our place in this world is conditioned by an underlying memory of continental outline.

Today, the outline of the North American coast is imprinted on our minds like the features of an old acquaintance. The thumb of Florida, the scalloped and chiselled cameo of Quebec, the loose cap of the Arctic islands pointing poleward, the extended palm of Alaska, the sockets of Hudson Bay and the Gulf of Mexico are clues to an unmistakable identity.

It was not always so. For nearly five centuries until well into the present one, the practice of following the line of the coast and translating it onto a map was the first task of many famous sea captains. One can imagine what excitement, after many weeks at sea, early seafarers must have felt at the first sighting of the coast.

The first who, in popular myth, "discovered" North America left thin clues about their whereabouts. Christopher Columbus, arriving in the Bahamas (never actually encountering the continental mainland), and John Cabot, five years later landing somewhere in Labrador, Newfoundland or Cape Breton, had no maps on which to fix a reference, nor the means (developed 250 years later) to accurately determine longitude.

In 1524, Giovanni da Verrazzano, sailing from South Carolina north past Newfoundland on his return to France, was the first to recognize that the coast was contiguous all the way from Florida, and that it was a part of a New World. A decade later, France's Jacques Cartier found the grand entrance to North America in the tapering estuary of the St. Lawrence which permitted sailing a thousand miles into the interior. The Spaniards explored California and Oregon from Mexican ports in the 1540s, and maps from the end of the century show the rough triangle of the continent, distorted but vaguely recognizable.

Detailed knowledge of the Pacific side of that triangle, however, lagged far behind that of the Atlantic. Only relatively recent and tentative expeditions, mostly Spanish and Russian, had ventured to the northwest coast when Cook, the preeminent navigator of his day, arrived off the coast of Oregon from Hawaii and sailed up to Alaska and around to the Bering Strait. By then, some of our east coast cities had been founded and the American Revolution was two years old. Another decade and a half would pass before the northwest would be surveyed in detail, establishing that most of it was a close-packed archipelago with numerous large islands fronting a maze of deep channels and fjords, and that hopeful rumors of an entrance there to a northwest passage were unfounded.

The search for such a passage dominated exploration of the third Arctic coast of North America; a three-century-long quest that claimed several hundred lives. Henry Hudson, having navigated through fog, ice floes and contrary currents to discover, in 1610, the big bay that bears his name, was abandoned there by a crew turned mutinous after overwintering. A few years later, Jens Munk entered the bay with two ships, lost over sixty men to scurvy, and returned to Denmark with only two other survivors. Many other expeditions continued to poke away at a network of ice-choked possibilities until Sir John Franklin almost completed the passage via Victoria Strait. Not one of Franklin's men survived to report the near-success after the expedition became icebound and Franklin died.

The search for Franklin, conducted by numerous admirals, and per-

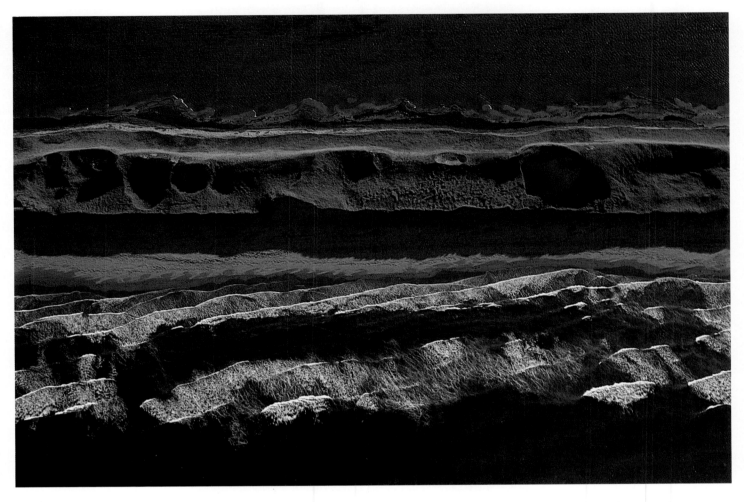

An aerial view along the north coast of Prince Edward Island. Grasses stabilize the dunes of a sandbar, which in turn protects a calm bay from breakers off the Gulf of St. Lawrence.

haps the greatest rescue effort ever mounted in the history of exploration, filled out many of the missing geographic details of the continent's last coast. But it was not until 1916 that Vilhjalmur Stefansson, traveling by skis rather than by ship, discovered the last significant islands in the vast Arctic Archipelago, which contains six of the world's thirty largest isles. And not until after aerial surveys following the Second World War was the map of North America, showing every last mile of the continent's remarkable coast, finally complete.

Today, the margins of North America still hold much to be discovered, although the process has been reversed; now archaeologists look for what they can discover about the explorers. Divers probe sunken wrecks from the Arctic to the Caribbean. Navigational detectives attempt to retrace the routes of ancient mariners. Nine different islands, for example, have been put forward as the first landfall made by Columbus; a 1986 analysis makes a strong case for uninhabited Samana Cay in the Bahamas.

We are now almost certain that 500 years before Columbus, the Norse reached the New World. They left ruins and relics rather than records, most notably at L'Anse aux Meadows along the northernmost tip of Newfoundland. Some have speculated that Basque fishermen, Irish Monks and even Romans preceded Columbus. Particularly strong cultural correspondences point to the likelihood of trans-Pacific voyages from Asia and Indonesia to the Mexican, South American and even northwestern coasts as long as several thousand years ago.

In absolute terms, the European "discovery" of North American shores belongs to the realm of map publishing. The coasts didn't need to be discovered by the Amerindians and Inuit who already lived there, and who had their own maps, transmitted by temporary tracings and preserved in memory.

Several hundred generations ago, when the ancestors of these people are assumed to have settled the continent, the coastlines were very different. Sea levels were several hundred feet lower on account of huge quantities of water held in continental ice sheets. It has long been assumed that, after crossing the broad expanse of dry land then connecting Alaska and Siberia, the Pleistocene ancestors of native Americans traveled to the heart of the continent across a glacier-free corridor just east of the Rocky Mountains. A new hypothesis, however, suggests that they may have moved down a more hospitable route along the exposed continental shelf on the Alaska and British Columbia coast. If correct, the second theory implies a potential for interesting finds for undersea archaeologists.

The coasts of North America harbor latent surprises in other fields, especially in the geosciences. What, for instance, are we to make of the near-perfect portion of a circle that cleanly indents half of the east side of Hudson Bay? Some propose that it is the outline of a huge old meteorite crater. It is also suggested that Hudson Bay itself is the basin of an even bigger, more ancient crater. Both ideas await proof.

This meteorite hypothesis is not particularly radical in comparison to a theory provoked by coastal shapes early in this century. A close fit had been noticed between the northwest shoulder of Africa and the eastern seaboard of North America, and between the elbow of South America and the facing

waist of Africa. The idea of jostling continents was subsequently derided by most scientists, but decades later turned out to be incontestibly correct. The lines of coasts had pointed the way to what eventually became one of the most remarkable revelations of science, one that would change forever how we look at the land, and at the great water-filled basins that border it.

Na Pali Coast, Kauai, Hawaiian Islands. At Hanakapiai Beach, boulders slick with seaweed mark the passage of high tide.

A shrimp fleet at anchor in Gulfport, Mississippi. Gulf coast cities in Mississippi boast deepwater ports, a shipbuilding industry and impressive natural shorelines.

Highrise buildings of Miami, Florida are mirrored in the still water at dawn.

1

W A T E R

EARTH, A RESPLENDENT BLUE AND WHITE AGAINST A BLACK
void, is the water planet. Water, despite its great abundance, is magic.

We seldom think of it as magic. We ingest it daily, wash with it and
flush large amounts of it down our drains. But water, the simple and sole
product of the explosive combination of two elemental gases, has a nearly
endless number of unique and extraordinary properties.

Water is the only substance we commonly encounter in all three states:
solid, liquid and vapor. Fantastic ferns of frost on a windowpane are made
of water, as are rainbows and Himalayan-size clouds. So, in fact, are we —
some ninety percent of us — as are most life-forms.

With a poet's eye, William Blake saw "a world in a grain of sand." Had
he looked instead at a bead of water with a scientist's tools, he might have
been more inspired. A single unsterilized drop of water can teem with

*In the blue, predawn light, the Na Pali
cliffs rise straight from the sea at
Kalalau Beach, Kauai Island, Hawaii.*

hundreds of microscopic creatures, a world of abundance and complexity one would never have suspected.

At the opposite end of the scale, few could fail to be awed by the fluid immensity that confronts us at the coast. Once, perceiving a flat world, people speculated on what kind of fantastic, frightening end it led to. Now we can imagine leaving from any point on the outer coast to sail completely around the planet, and return, perhaps, without once seeing land. Amidst the globe-circling oceans, our continents are but large islands.

Perhaps even more compelling than the ungraspable extent of the sea is its restlessness. Forever in motion, its waves, tides and currents are manifest most dramatically along the coast. Waves, the complex progeny of wind (in turn the offspring of the sun and the earth's rotation), are especially powerful off the Pacific between California and British Columbia, perhaps the highest energy coastline in the world. With the greatest potential "fetch," (the distance over which the wind acts), across the world's widest ocean, swells dragged by the prevailing westerlies strike the curved belly of the continent dead-on, cresting into spectacular breakers as they reach the shoals.

The breakers driven in by winter storms are the most violent. Cars, several dozen feet up on bluffs overlooking the water, can be overturned. Tillamook Lighthouse in Oregon, 139 feet above sea level, has to be protected by steel bars from hundred-pound rocks that the sea sometimes hurls up.

The arrival of storm swells on the coast brings out admirers, some of whom try to get as close as possible to the monster surf. Once in a while someone miscalculates, misjudges the size of an incoming giant and, unable to outrun the onrushing deluge, is lost to the heaving maelstrom.

While large waves are commonly accompanied by their winds, swells can undulate across tremendous distances on their own. In one case, sophisticated monitoring tracked waves from their point of generation in a storm, in the southern Indian Ocean, all the way to the south coast of Alaska, a distance of 12,000 miles.

A different kind of wave, not related to wind, occasionally strikes the coast. Tsunami, the propagated shocks of earthquake or volcanic explosion, are rare but potentially deadly. Travelling at 450 miles per hour, several dozen miles long and scarcely a foot high, they are unnoticeable on the open ocean. Approaching shore, they slow, shorten and gain height. If the configuration of the coast allows, they may be focused to heights of a hundred feet. A series of tsunami once killed a hundred thousand people in Japan. They are a concern in Hawaii, but rarely threaten our mainland. In 1964, however, several people on a northern California beach were drowned by tsunami from the Alaska Earthquake.

Alaska holds the record for the most enormous wave ever recorded, one that reared higher than the Empire State Building. This one came from the land, rather than the sea. Late on the evening of July 9, 1958, on the Pacific side of the impressive Fairweather Range, an earthquake precipitated a landslide into a fjord at the head of Lituya Bay. An estimated ninety million tons of rock smashed off the snout of the tidewater glacier below and threw up a wave that reached nearly two thousand feet high on nearby slopes, mowing millions of trees from the surrounding landscape into the bay. Three fishing boats, anchored at the entrance to the bay, were confronted with a huge oncoming mountain of water; the crews of two of them managed to survive.

On the Atlantic coast, the equivalent of a mountain of water is moved twice a day in and out of the Bay of Fundy, where tidal ranges of more than sixty feet occur. At the forked head of the bay, scores of square miles of slick, reddish-brown mud flats are exposed when the outgoing tide evacuates Chignecto Bay, Cobequid Bay and Minas Basin. While the tides here are high, some claim slightly higher range for Leaf Basin, off Ungava Bay in northern Quebec, while several other long bays in the eastern Arctic also have enormous tidal ranges.

While the east coast has the world's largest tides, the west can probably claim the world's fastest tidal currents. Among the glacier-cut waterways of British Columbia are several places where extensive inlets are connected to the sea by a narrow passage. The waters draining through such constrictions, in places such as Skookumchuck Narrows and the mouth of Seymour Inlet, can create foaming city-block-size whirlpools and turbulent tidal rapids.

The place where stream and sea meet is a different environment of its own, distinct from river and ocean. In some cases, the meeting is a wide, deep estuary, a mingling of river current and tide, and of fresh and salty water. Trenched by continental glaciers during the ice ages, such are the estuaries of the St. Lawrence and its tributary, the Saguenay River. Here, between prominent banks, there are tides and whales, both sometimes larger than their counterparts along the open coast. At Quebec City, which lies more than two hundred miles from the nearest point on the Atlantic, the tidal range is eighteen feet.

Some rivers end their journey in the intricate unburdening of a delta. So ends the Mississippi. Over a period of sixty million years, it has dropped an enormous amount of sediment at its mouth and over the floodplain upstream. In fact, the Mississippi Delta is but the tip of a mostly submerged fan, a wide mound eight miles high and three hundred in radius sitting on the floor of the Gulf of Mexico. The accumulated weight of the deposits of the floodplain and deltaic fan has formed a tremendous sag in the earth's crust, a testament to the hydrologic cycle. In the course of its long existence, enough water has discharged through the mouth of the Mississippi to fill all the oceans in the world several times over.

More awesome at least on the surface are the deltas of the two greatest northern rivers, the Yukon and the Mackenzie. The latter, in particular, is mind-boggling when viewed from the air: a net of hundreds of channels and more than ten thousand lakes and ponds covering several thousand square miles.

But perhaps the most spectacular sections of the coast are those that meet glacial ice. In Alaska, numerous glaciers reach tidewater, terminating in cracked, jagged, blue-and-white cliffs from which large blocks and occasional towers and walls of ice calve noisily into berg-choked inlets. Places like Glacier Bay, Yakutat Bay and Prince William Sound with its famous Columbia Glacier are renowned for their elemental and awesome scenery.

Bigger glaciers calving much bigger icebergs are found off the west coast of Greenland. After being carried first north, then south on a three-year journey in the looping Labrador current, these splendid, white, float-

ing mountains appear off the coast of Newfoundland, sometimes reaching the latitude of New England and even the Carolinas. An exceptional one may tower as much as three hundred feet above the surface, which is just the tip of it, of course, eighty-five percent being below the water.

The icebergs, in turn, are but punctuation marks in the forbidding fantasy that is our Arctic coast. Motionless, the Arctic is the only ocean that is predominantly frozen. When the ice pack breaks up in summer, the shifting tides leave wrecked floes strewn along the shore, each a carved blue marvel like some glossy Inuit sculpture.

Meanwhile, the cold currents descending from the Arctic and encountering warmer air make parts of the east coast, especially from Newfoundland northward, the foggiest places in the world. From mists, to innumerable towers of grand cumulus sailing across blue skies, to a far distant horizon and beyond, water in its vaporous form also joins in the magic moving show of the coast.

A wave explodes near one of the openings in the Sea Lion Caves, Oregon. Hecate Head Lighthouse is visible in the distance.

LEFT:

Mackenzie Delta, Northwest Territories. This aerial view shows just a small portion of the maze of channels and ponds that constitute one of the largest river deltas in the world.

OVERLEAF:

A hiker walks the glassy, broad beach at Nels Bight near Cape Scott, the wild northwestern tip of Vancouver Island, British Columbia.

*Viewed from cliffs, silky waves slip
among rock forms on a beach in Big Sur.*

A lone beacon marks the route of safe passage around the many rocks at Montana De Oro State Park, California.

All along the port of Savannah, Georgia,
the Gulf Stream brings warm water
from the tropics, moderating
temperatures on land.

The #10 Highway over Mobile Bay in Alabama. Mobile is the busy port city of the Tennessee-Tombigbee Waterway.

Atlantic surf breaks on the rocks at the base of a cliff at twilight. A long photographic exposure creates the misty effect.

In the blue of evening shade, a small waterfall cascades onto a beach on Grand Manan Island near the entrance to the Bay of Fundy.

A brisk wind blows the spray from the crest of a wave at Point Reyes Beach, Point Reyes National Seashore, California.

Brandywine Falls is one of hundreds of waterfalls in the Coast Mountains of British Columbia.

*A glacier descends from the Fairweather
Range to tidewater in Glacier Bay
National Park, Alaska.*

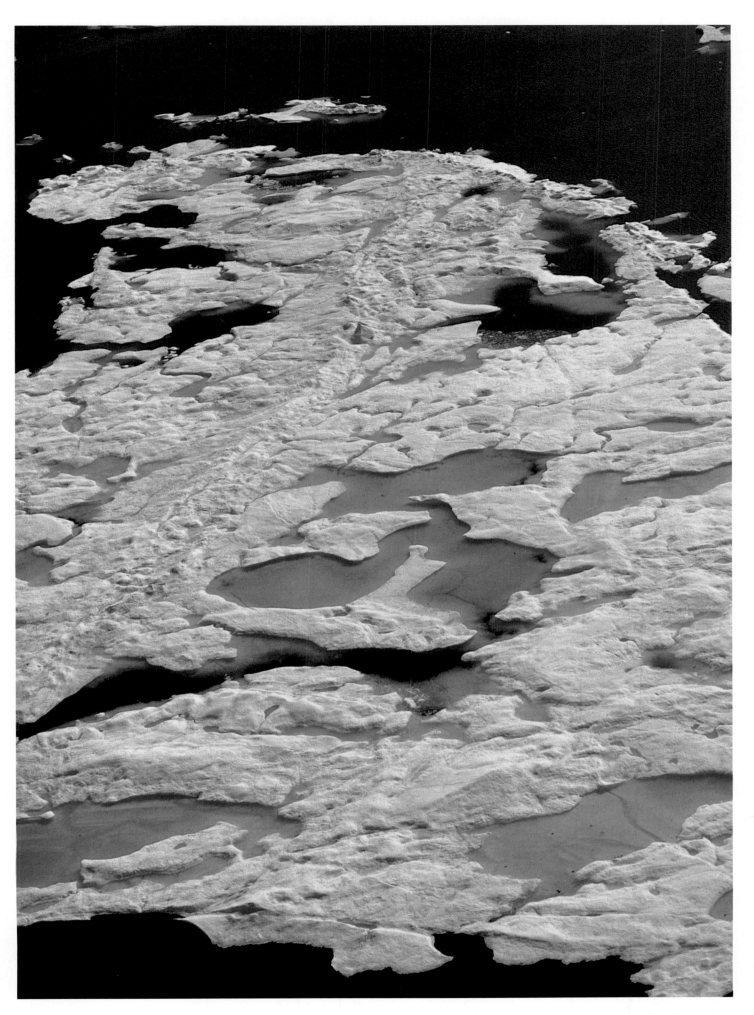

*Seen from the air, an ice floe in Arctic
waters slowly melts in August.*

The view south of the Big Sur coastline, California.

High cliffs provide an ideal vantage for watching sets of waves roll ashore at Jalama Beach, California, a favorite spot for surfboarders.

34

After a winter storm, violent waves smash the windward coast at Waianapanapa State Park, Maui, Hawaii.

Waves from the open ocean rush up a surge channel near Wya Point, Pacific Rim National Park, British Columbia.

A fishing pier at Thimble Shoal in Chesapeake Bay stretches out into the 200-mile-long estuary. Salt water from the Atlantic Ocean and fresh water from 150 rivers combine to create a unique environment for over 2,500 species of plants and animals.

*The Florida Keys extend from Key Largo
to Key West and touch upon such towns
as Perky, Big Pine Key and Tavernier.*

2

L A N D

THE VAST SEA, MADE OF ONE SUBSTANCE ESSENTIALLY
unchanged during a several billion-year dominance of the planet, is awesome in its uniformity. Land, on the other hand, is amazing in its material
diversity, and in its complex past. How the sea behaves and why, the
workings of moon and tide, the rhythms of wind and wave and current,
have been apparent in principle for centuries. How the land really behaves
has only been known for little more than three decades, and why is still a
matter of considerable speculation.

   Pick up one of the variegated, wave-shuffled, polished pebbles on a
beach and you have in your hand a story involving millions, perhaps
billions of years of remarkable change. You may hold a seasoned traveler,
something that has moved hundreds or maybe many thousands of miles.
Though the pebble may be a remnant of some hill that once existed close to
where you stand, where you stand has moved thousands of miles across the

*The inland seaway of the Strait of
Georgia runs between Vancouver Island,
here on the distant horizon, and the
British Columbia mainland, where the
Coast Mountains descend to the water's
edge.*

surface of the planet during its not too distant past.

If the pebble was picked up from a beach somewhere on the northeast coast and if, as is likely there, it came from rock more than 200 million years old, it is certain that in its earliest history it was not near the Atlantic. Two hundred million years ago the Atlantic Ocean did not exist. If the pebble was instead from any Pacific beach, it is likely that its origins were not on the North American continent.

In retrospect, it now seems obvious why, for example, the west coast is backed everywhere by relatively young, growing mountains, while in the east there are only old, worn-down ones. But it wasn't until the 1960s, after evidence was brought up from the bottoms of the oceans, that the idea of continental drift was proved to be fact, and the newborn science of plate tectonics began to explain how it worked.

We now know that the earth's lithosphere, its thin outer layer carrying the continents together with the rock bottoms of the oceans, is divided into several irregularly-shaped plates, somewhat like the close-fitting sections of a fractured eggshell. The plates are continually moving. Along the edges of the plates, new material is added to the lithosphere; where they collide, a corresponding amount of material must disappear into the underlying mantle as one plate descends under the other, a process called subduction.

Two different types of rock make up the earth's thin shell. Denser, basaltic rock lines the deep ocean basins. In contrast, the continental base rocks, granitic in composition, form a thicker crust which, being less dense, essentially "floats" higher on the underlying, plastic mantle.

The western half of the Atlantic Basin, together with the American continents, make up the North and South American plates. The eastern half of the Atlantic Basin, together with Eurasia and Africa respectively, constitute two more plates. For several dozen million years now, the Atlantic Ocean has been getting wider, and the North and South American plates have been moving west, away from Eurasia and Africa, and colliding with oceanic plates under the Pacific. The tremendous chain of mountain ranges that runs from Alaska to Tierra del Fuego is simply the result of this slow-motion crash.

The westward moving edge of North America is its active margin. Earthquakes, volcanoes and all the large scale features of the Pacific coastline follow from that fact. The Atlantic coast is the passive margin; away from the front end of the collision, nothing much is happening to it at this time.

Right down the middle of the Atlantic runs the mid-Atlantic ridge, a staggered crack which marks the division between the opposite moving plates. As the sea floor spreads apart along this rift, hot magma rises from below, elevating the ridge and adding new lithosphere to the receding ocean floor on either side.

It all leads back to age-old stories of breathtaking proportions. Two hundred million years ago the Americas, Eurasia and Africa were all a single supercontinent called Pangea. The rift that marked the slow split-up of this vast landmass is the one now in the mid-Atlantic. Between it and North America's east coast — which once lay in the high interior of Pangea — a two thousand-mile-wide trailing section of ocean floor has been added to the North American plate.

Thus the east coast, now actually in the middle of the North American plate is geologically quiet. From Mexico to Long Island, it is a low-lying coastal plain, made of relatively young sedimentary rock generally less than sixty-five million years old.

Pangea itself was the result of the continents coming together at an earlier time. The northern Appalachians were thrust skyward to Himalayan heights as North America rammed Europe some 440 million years ago. Today, the Atlantic laps at the worn-down stumps of the northern Appalachians along the coast from New England to Newfoundland. From Cadillac Mountain, in Maine's Acadia National Park, the view leads down gently forested hills, across a network of bays and green islands and out to sea. A few hundred years ago, the scene resembled the cold, stark, jagged view from the summit of Mount Everest.

That's not all, of course. Earlier, between 680 and 520 million years ago, before it crunched into Euro-Africa, North America ran into and broke up a micro-continent called Avalonia. The original rock from this land can now be found in scattered places on opposite coasts of the Atlantic: in Massachusetts, along the New Brunswick side of the Bay of Fundy, in Cape Breton, throughout the Avalon Peninsula of Newfoundland, in Southern Ireland and Northern Wales. That beach pebble in your hand has not only traveled far, but may have an identical, long-separated twin on the other side of the ocean.

All of North America, westward from the Rocky Mountains along the present Continental Divide to the coast, is believed to consist of "suspect terrains," which originated in places other than where they are now found. Before the Atlantic opened up, the opposite side of the continent was missing almost all of Alaska, British Columbia, Washington, Oregon and California, as well as parts of adjacent states and western Mexico. Tracing back the geological origins of Pacific North America is a putting Humpty-Dumpty-back-together-again problem that will preoccupy geologists for decades to come. Among the remarkable details that have been determined is the fact that building blocks for the Wrangell-St. Elias Mountains, the great coastal ranges of Alaska, likely came from some place in the South Pacific.

Meanwhile, the Pacific plate continues to withdraw under Alaska, generating the stress and heat that has created the volcanic arc of the Aleutian Islands. And far to the south, it is dragging California west of the San Andreas fault towards Alaska, resulting in terrible earthquakes.

Through all the collisions that have added pieces to and rearranged the margins of North America, one part of the continent, known as the craton, remains its nucleus. Here, the rock is a billion, sometimes two billion years old. This is the Canadian Shield, and it is exposed along virtually the entire coast of Quebec and most of the coasts of Baffin Island and the mainland of the Northwest Territories. While continental coastlines are among the most rapidly changing landscapes on earth, and therefore are young, this says nothing about the rock of which they are made. In the similar shield landscape of the west coast of Greenland, rock formed over three billion years ago has been found.

While there are fundamental differences between the east and the west coasts of North America, the contrast between the northern and the southern coasts is, in some ways, even greater.

Whereas in the lower forty-eight states and in southernmost Canada, roads follow the coast and are never far from it, no roads run parallel to the coast of most of British Columbia, southern Alaska or Labrador. No roads ever will. These coasts are so severely incised with long, deep fjords that any highways along them would be unthinkably costly and incredibly circuitous. The creation of such convoluted coastlines was the result of processes that spanned a period of only one or two million years, instead of a hundred million. During the ice ages, virtually all of Canada, and some points south, were covered with thick ice caps. This glaciation carved out the fjords and also left great moraines at the melting ice front, debris that forms the great hook of Cape Cod and the nearby islands of Nantucket and Martha's Vineyard.

The Pleistocene glaciations, which so profoundly shaped the northern coasts, and indeed half of the entire continent, represent processes of erosion, a completely different kind of land shaping from anything caused by the movement of plates. And yet, the two are connected, for the continental glaciation could not have occurred but for the northern position that North America has drifted into. Only 400 million years ago, it straddled the Equator.

Walking the beach, one can marvel at the power of the onrushing waves which carved the cliffs, isolated the sea stacks, deposited the beaches and polished the pebbles. Looking inland at a mountain, one can imagine it as a huge, slow wave: rising on forces in the earth, falling as erosion grinds it down, advancing forward as the continent moves. From a human perspective, it is a slow process. In its own way, on its own time, however, the land is as fluid and as restless as the sea.

The Florida Everglades has been described as a curving, sluggish "river of grass" only inches deep. Its tropical conditions give rise to small islands of hardwood forest.

The sea reveals a beach of polished pebbles in Montana De Oro State Park, California.

Wave-polished stone glows in the last rays of the day at Cabo San Lucas, the very tip of the Baja Peninsula, Mexico.

OVERLEAF:

Howe Sound, British Columbia, at dusk. From Vancouver north through the Alaska Panhandle lies a coast of tall evergreens, and innumerable winding bays, inlets and passages.

Grasses stabilize an expanse of sand dunes at Cape Cod, Massachusetts.

Wind-sculpted waves of sand stretch right to the shoreline at Pismo Beach State Park, California.

Sea stacks abound in Olympic National Park, Washington, which contains the wildest coastline in the lower forty-eight states. These stacks stand a day's walk from the road.

A fine group of sea stacks is the main feature of Ecola State Park in northern Oregon.

The sun streams through a hole in a sea arch at Big Sur Beach, California.

A crashing wave obscures the setting sun at Cabo San Lucas, Baja, Mexico.

*Long Island, New York. New York City
is situated in a natural harbor of bays
and rivers, such as the Hudson River
which flows past Long Island.*

Myrtle Beach, South Carolina. The tropical climate and convivial culture of the Sunbelt along the southeast coast attract tens of millions of tourists a year.

As it hardens, fast-flowing surface lava leaves a ropy, wave-like pattern which can be seen throughout Volcanoes National Park.

Exposed by the pounding of waves, colored layers of rock strata lie along the coastline in Montana De Oro State Park.

58

The view looking westward from Inspiration Point on east Anacapa Island, eleven miles off the California coast in the Channel Islands National Park.

Surrounded by the sea, the famous monolith of Percé Rock, Quebec, was once part of the mainland.

*The Na Pali Cliffs on Kauai, Hawaii,
recede into the distance as sunlight hits
the salt spray.*

*Ground fog hangs in the valleys at
sunrise, Point Reyes National Seashore,
California.*

3

CYCLE

IN NATURE, EVERYTHING IS LINKED IN SOME WAY TO A CYCLE. The earth loops the sun, spinning, and is chased by the moon. Seasons rotate, winds whirl, currents circulate. There is night and day, death and birth, ebb and flow, endless change and eternal return.

Perhaps no other place is as evocative of these cycles as the coast where one can watch the sun rise or set behind the sea and the tides advance and withdraw, while the weather turns in the distant sky.

And then there is the rotation of the water itself — the swirl of entire oceans in broad, global gyres. The three generally clockwise-moving spirals in the Northern Hemisphere have profound effects on our coasts. In particular, climate is greatly modified by certain warm or cold currents, which are spinoffs of the Arctic, the North Pacific or the North Atlantic Gyre.

Part of the last, the Gulf Stream is the best known. Warm, westward-flowing tropical currents enter the Caribbean and exit after further warm-

On a rock off the Baja Peninsula, a pelican prunes its feathers against a shimmering ocean.

ing. The swift-flowing current, forty miles wide and 3,300 feet deep, parallels the coast from Florida to Cape Hatteras, North Carolina, and heads northeast back across the Atlantic, where it acts as the cause of northern Europe's mild winters. The Atlantic coast of Maine and that of Spain are at comparable latitudes, and yet the contrast in their climate is great. The differences are made even more pronounced by the Labrador current which brings cold Arctic water down the northeast coast.

Meanwhile, the North Pacific equivalent to the Gulf Stream, the Kuroshio Extension, brings mild temperatures to the northwest coast, from California to southern Alaska. The combination of relatively warm water and prevailing westerly winds — as well as a high mountain barrier — makes this part of the coast the rainiest and, at higher altitudes, snowiest region in North America. Places on the west side of the Olympic Peninsula, Washington, for example, have received more than 200 inches of precipitation in a year.

The mild, wet climate has prompted the growth of the stateliest forests on earth, where trees as tall as a twenty-story office building are common, and where at least three species, Douglas fir, Sitka spruce and California redwood sometimes exceed 300 feet in height.

South from this rain coast the climate gets rapidly drier. From southernmost California, down the length of the Baja Peninsula, there exists, at the opposite extreme, one of the driest regions on the continent. Here, the prevailing winds swing away from the land, and the offshore current, containing water that has welled up from deeper regions, is relatively cold and has a stabilizing effect on air masses. The weather of the Baja coast is among the most consistent and pleasant anywhere.

Again, for something completely different, one has simply to follow the same line of latitude across to the Atlantic coast, where in Florida the most violent possible weather is a serious threat. Tornadoes sometimes occur, but the region is best known for its hurricanes. Breeding in the tropical Atlantic, where warmth and water vapor feed tremendous energy into their whorling masses, hurricanes follow the groove of the same atmospheric circulation that pushes the gyre. By the time they hit the coast, these concentrated, spinning storms commonly produce sustained winds exceeding a hundred miles per hour.

Climatological cycles account for most of the biological differences between otherwise comparable coasts. The swamps of the Florida Everglades have only latitude in common with the desert dunes and cacti of Baja. The same can be said for the barren, stony fjords of Labrador when compared to the water corridors of the Alaska Panhandle, which are immured with thick carpets of forest.

As the terrestrial biology of the coast is linked to these spirals of water, so is the marine. A moving ocean is a fertile one. Upwelling cold currents bring oxygen and nutrients to warmer waters, causing explosive growth in plankton and in the populations of other marine life up the food pyramid.

The California current, turning southward from the Kuroshio Extension (the north veering fork becomes the warm Alaska current), is such a cold stream. Meanwhile, just off the coast at Monterey, the Monterey Canyon acts like a funnel on landward tendrils of the current, creating conditions for a tremendous quantity and diversity of marine life. Vast schools of sardines once swam here in seemingly inexhaustible abundance.

Seine boats once brought their slippery silver harvest to feed the fish plants at Cannery Row. The sardines and their accompanying industry disappeared in the 1940s because of overfishing.

The greatest of North American fishing grounds are the Grand Banks on the continental shelf off Newfoundland. Water comes in mainly from the cold Labrador current while the Gulf Stream skirts the southern edge of the banks. Haddock, redfish, halibut, mackerel, herring and, most abundant of all, cod feed here in great numbers.

Many fish in the sea migrate with the currents of the ocean gyres, in synchrony with seasonal food cycles. Migration is another grand cycle that is manifested most dramatically along the coasts. More compelling than the unseen movements of schools offshore is the mass movement of fish between sea and continent. The spawning migration of different species of salmon on both the Atlantic and Pacific coasts, but especially on the latter, signals a feast for bird, beast and man alike. In season, grizzly bears gather at choice spots to catch the salmon, each fish returning to the same stream and sometimes to the very same gravel bar, where it was born. The American eel lives a similar life cycle in reverse, dwelling in freshwater rivers of the Atlantic, returning at the end of its life to its spawning grounds in the Sargasso Sea, a current-free mid-ocean region of seaweed encircled by the North Atlantic gyre.

The coast is witness to many other kinds of migrations. Many north-south bird flyways follow the coastline. Numerous seabirds, on the other hand, move between the land and the sea. Gannets, fulmars, guillemots, murres, kittiwakes, puffins and other species spend many months at sea, away from land. They return to seacliffs and isolated islands to nest in spectacular colonies.

Marine mammals, such as sea lions, fur seals, elephant seals and walrus, swim to secluded places on the coasts to breed and to give birth. The longest mammal migration in the world is the 15,000-mile round-trip made by California gray whales between the cold Bering Sea off Alaska and their winter breeding grounds in the warm lagoons of Baja. In February, in the Laguna San Ignacio, their spouts are sometimes numerous enough to resemble a vaporous picket fence on the horizon.

Meanwhile, man has thrown monkey wrenches into the cycles. Relentless exploitation, in the form of hunting and habitat destruction, has eliminated some species and greatly reduced the numbers of many of the rest. The flightless great auk, one of the most impressive of the seabirds of the North Atlantic, was clubbed to extinction in the last century. Walrus once ranged far south of their present range, and could be found on the Magdalen Islands in the Gulf of St. Lawrence. What was once an extraordinary abundance of life has been so diminished that one writer calls it "The Sea of Slaughter." In fact, according to some estimates, the amount of life in the world's oceans as a whole has been rapidly reduced to half.

The sea has a great regenerative capacity. In fact, in recent decades, protected populations of sea otters, sea lions and sea elephants have increased along the Pacific coast. Sardines are again being fished off Monterey, though in nowhere near the same quantities as in former times.

But simply restricting what may be taken from the coast may not be enough. As the infamous case of the *Exxon Valdez* oil spill showed, we have a tremendous capacity to destroy environments inadvertently. Despite a cleanup costing over a billion dollars, tens of thousands of birds and thousands of mammals were found to be affected, with long-term damage still unknown. The disaster was just the best known of many incidents. A few months later, in a much less publicized case, more than ten thousand oil-covered seabirds washed up on the coast of Newfoundland, the source and location of the slick, undetermined. Most likely, it resulted from the criminal actions of a tanker illegally flushing its bilges while at sea.

One of the key cycles in nature, the hydrological cycle, drops several thousand cubic miles of rain and snow on the continent each year. Returning to sea, the rivers bring down nutrients to the spawning grounds of most commercial fish estuaries. Now, however, rivers bring poison as well, from industry, sewage and agriculture runoff. Apart from lethal heavy metals, pesticides and other chemicals, nitrogen and phosphorous found in fertilizers provoke algae blooms which consume the oxygen in the water, causing mass suffocation of fish. In the St. Lawrence River, because of the great amount of pollution, the future looks very bleak for the beluga and blue whales that visit there.

All kinds of garbage is dumped into the ocean. It has been estimated that merchant fleets alone throw about five million plastic containers overboard each year. Large, industrial cities take their garbage and sewage and release it a hundred miles offshore. As a result, as many as two million seabirds and a hundred thousand mammals die every year after eating or becoming entangled with debris. Sea turtles choke on plastic bags mistaken for jellyfish, sea lions starve with plastic rings around their mouths and pelicans, entangled in nets, end up hung from trees. Harbor seals and fish with ulcerous lesions are becoming more common. In the last three years, over a thousand dolphins with blisters, craters and huge patches of skin sloughed off have been found dead or dying on the Atlantic coast.

Meanwhile, sections of the Long Island coast, among others, have had to be closed in recent years as balls of raw sewage, syringes and other medical waste began to accumulate on the beaches.

Eventually, it all washes back up on shore.

A flock of gulls congregates on a beach on Florida's Gulf coast.

*Low tide reveals a group of sea stars and
sea anemones on a remote beach in
Olympic National Park, Washington.*

Exposed at low tide, a sea star displays its vivid colors at Point Lobos State Reserve, California.

A gannet carries seaweed back to its nest on Bonaventure Island near Percé, Quebec.

A familiar sight along the Florida coast, a common egret stoically waits for its meal in the wash along a beach.

Once a year at Año Nuevo, California, elephant seals come to shore to bear young and breed. They spend nearly three months on land without eating or drinking.

A female elephant seal tosses cool sand onto her back while lolling in the hot midday sun.

*A migrating gray whale passes the
Channel Islands en route to its breeding
grounds off the Baja Peninsula.*

Gulls gather to feed where a small stream fans across a beach near Netarts, Oregon.

Queen Charlotte Islands, British Columbia. Mist veils virgin forests of age-old cedar and Sitka spruce.

With abundant sunshine and rain, the hillsides along the Hana coast of Maui, Hawaii, are covered with a thick canopy of trees.

In small groves of eucalyptus trees along the California coast, migrating monarch butterflies gather as they fly south to Mexico.

*Cape St. Mary's Bird Sanctuary,
Newfoundland. Behind the scores of
seabirds in flight, hundreds more can be
seen nesting on the shady cliff face.*

*Sunlight filters through misty glades on
Florida's Atlantic coast.*

PREVIOUS PAGES:

*Magnificent birds with six-foot
wingspans, gannets are part of a colony
of thirty thousand nesting seabirds at
Cape St. Mary's, Newfoundland.*

*With most of its roots exposed, a cypress
clings tenaciously to a cliff at Point
Lobos State Reserve, California.*

A crescent moon rises between the fronds of a coconut palm at Maui, Hawaii.

Evening silhouettes a screen of arbutus trees on Pender Island, British Columbia.

*An alligator emerges in marsh water
near Charleston, South Carolina.*

*Cypress Gardens near Charleston,
South Carolina.*

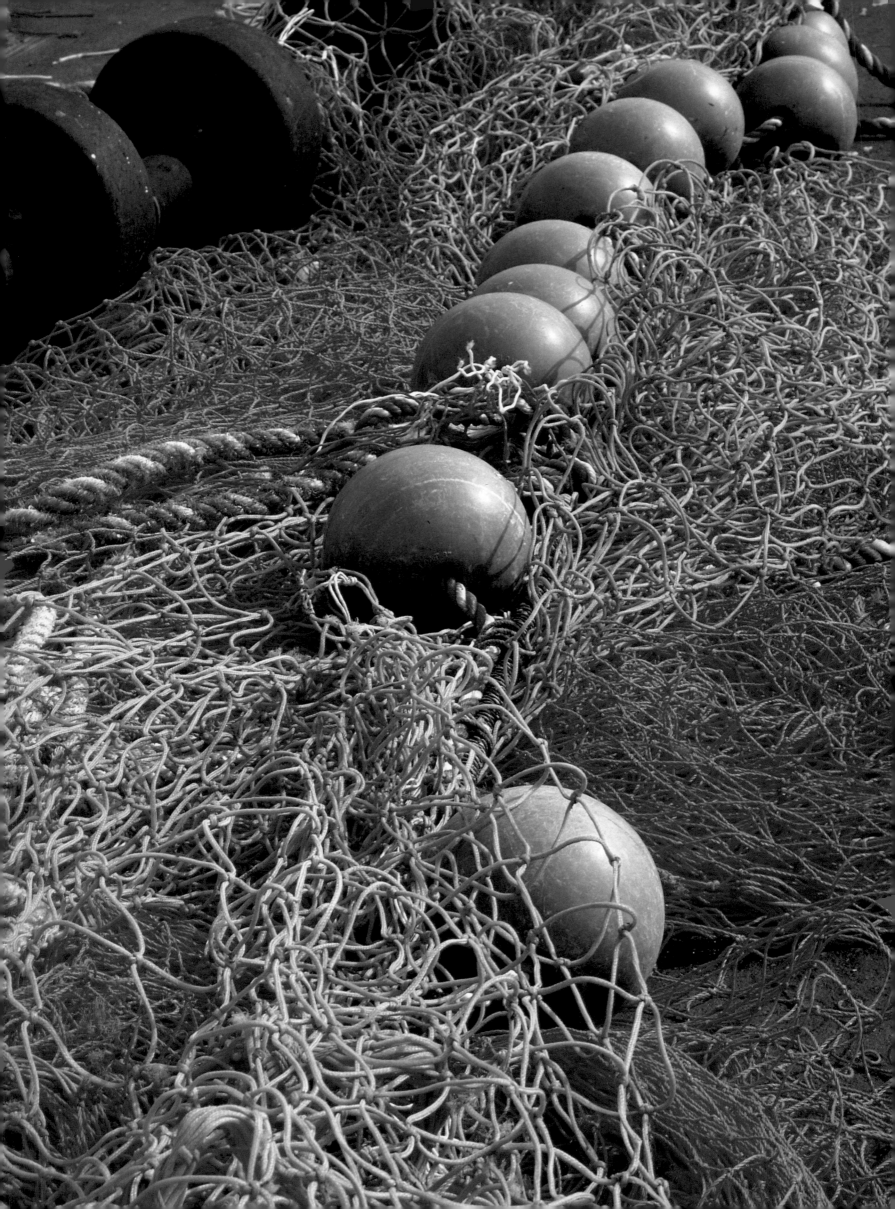

4

C O M M U N I T Y

ALONG THE COASTS OF NORTH AMERICA, NATURAL HARBORS
are innumerable, tucked around the bends of estuaries, located behind
barrier islands or sand banks and protected inside the stone gates of coves.
But relative to the length of the coast as a whole, they are uncommon. They
are the chosen places around which communities were destined to grow.

Perhaps nowhere else is a community more strongly fashioned by its
specific environment, as well as by the bond of commonality, than along
the coast. An agricultural town is mostly a visiting place and a center of
commerce for the farmers living in isolated homesteads scattered across the
surrounding fields. A logging or a mining town, apart from its impermanent
nature, has an arbitrary appearance. While the existence of the latter, for
example, is based on the proximity of mineral deposits, there is usually
nothing in the landscape that lends a sense of locality to such a community.

*Fishing nets and floats lie on a wharf at
Sable Island, Nova Scotia.*

Ineffably, coastal communities seem to be a part of their setting. The classic fishing village, ever a ready subject for calendar and postcard, is picturesque because it is harmonious; it has evolved in its place, rather than been imposed upon it.

Linked to the sea, the coastal community has as much to do with boats as it does with houses. The craft of boat design and construction, part and parcel of the heritage of the coast, is alive in many settlements. Along the coast of Maine, in Port Townsend off Puget Sound, Washington and in individual workshops on the islands to the north, wooden-boat building is pursued at the level of fine art. From Sable Island, Nova Scotia comes the fiberglass-hulled Cape Island boat, the well-known workhorse of the in-shore Atlantic fisheries. Even the simple, open and sturdy Newfoundland dory is a craft worthy of admiration and respect.

With form strictly following function, as well as efficiency of movement and durability, boat building is of necessity more demanding than simple house construction. The tradition of the discipline seems consistent with the neat, spare dignity of many coastal communities, especially on the Atlantic coast where simple, pastel clapboard and shingle dwellings are common.

Lunenburg, Nova Scotia is especially tidy and attractive, even when seen from the air, an angle that is unflattering to most towns. It is perhaps no coincidence that this port of German immigrants once built elegant sailing schooners, one of them, the *Bluenose*, the most famous fishing vessel of all time.

Of all coastal communities, none had more character than those of the Indian settlements along the northwest coast. With the sea on one side and rain forest on the other, Amerindians developed a lavish and sophisticated culture. Turn-of-the-century photographs show exotic scenes: beach-facing villages of sturdy longhouses fronted with a forest of stately totem poles; great sea-going canoes with high, elaborately-carved prows; quasi-religious ceremonies with dancers in colorful disguise wearing fantastic wooden masks.

There were dozens of quite distinct tribes, among them the Tlingit, Haida, Tsimshian, Kwakiutl, Salish, Nootka and Chinook. Common to all was the salmon, their most frequent dish in a predominantly fish diet. Northward from California, ritual ceremonies celebrated and revered the return to the rivers of the first salmon.

Also esteemed was the cedar, whose workable and durable wood was fashioned into many useful and decorative items, from simple utensils and thick massive planks, to exquisitely crafted canoes and totem poles. The latter, with their highly stylized representations of wildlife of the coast — eagle, bear, orca and raven — reflected a pride in ancestry and served primarily as emblems of family status. Keelless dugout canoes, burned and hewn out of a single trunk, were sometimes more than fifty feet long and eight wide.

The Nootka, in particular, living on Vancouver Island, and their off-shoot, the Makah on the Olympic Peninsula, made intrepid excursions to hunt the giant gray and humpback whales that cruised off the coast. The chief of the village organized thirty-foot, eight-man canoes for the hunt and took on the privilege of throwing the harpoon. This was attached to a cedar-bark rope, usually about a couple of hundred yards long with four sealskin floats attached at regular intervals. These would tire the harpooned whale and indicate its depth. If the dangerous plan succeeded, the perhaps forty-ton goliath would finally be dragged up on the beach in front of the chief's lodge. Whale songs would be sung, each distinctive to a family — an heirloom passed down along the generations.

A few Indian people alive today remember the songs their fathers and grandfathers sang. The whaling tradition goes back a long time; artifacts two thousand years old have been uncovered at a now abandoned camp at Cape Alava on the Washington coast. But the times of giant whales and giant trees are now gone.

The native northwest communities suffered great losses of their own numbers when white men arrived, carrying deadly diseases against which the Indian had no immunity. On the Queen Charlotte Islands, the Haida were reduced from a population of 8,000 to only 600 by 1900. Now, they number 1,500, and their culture seems secure in the hands of many talented artists. The striking, graphic language of their traditional art is expressed in many media, including silver jewelry, button-embroidered blankets, silk-screen prints, cedar boxes and masks, the occasional grand totem, and fine carvings made from argillite, a local black slate to which only the Haida have access.

For small communities along isolated stretches of coast, the attribute of resourcefulness seems self-evident, and perhaps nowhere more so than along the coast of Newfoundland. Confronting harsh and dangerous elements, the fishermen who live here epitomize self-reliance. Unlike most coastal inhabitants, they have little choice. The Newfoundland communities, their backs to a hard, empty landscape, must extract a livelihood from the sea or die.

Resourcefulness isn't enough when the resources are gone, today a tragic possibility for Newfoundlanders. Scientists have discovered that stocks of cod, the once superabundant staple of the Grand Banks, are alarmingly low, and already strict catch quotas must be reduced drastically. Thousands of people in the fisheries will lose their jobs. Worse, what has been one of the world's most important and prolific fishing grounds for centuries is turning into slim pickings, an ominous portent for the oceans as a whole.

Even before the present crisis, fishermen were being encouraged to leave their picturesque outports and move to larger towns with big fish plants. The tendency towards bigger, "more efficient" resource exploitation has been felt in other coastal regions as well. With boats capable of remaining at sea over longer periods, small coastal canneries on the British Columbia and Alaska coast have disappeared, and the population of outlying coastal areas has actually decreased in the last couple of decades.

Meanwhile, the population of coastal regions as a whole is increasing at a rapid rate, having doubled within the last four decades. Now, more than a third of the combined population of Canada and the United States lives within fifty miles of the coast. Many newcomers don't have the same understanding of the sea that resides in established communities. People in the Carolinas, Georgia and Oregon have built their seafront dream homes with an eye for the view, heedless of the fact that a single storm can completely alter the shoreline, forgetting that vehicles can destroy the stabilizing vegetation of coastal dunes, and suffering the consequences

Seaworthy boats lie at anchor in St. John's harbor. Overfishing threatens the way of life of Newfoundland's intrepid offshore fishermen.

Sunset over New York City provides a surreal mixture of pink and orange hues.

when their house, not to mention their land, is about to disappear.

Along a coast that is becoming increasingly crowded with naval bases, oil tanker ports and nuclear power plants, not to mention big cities, the coastal community is becoming more of an anachronism. But it offers an important example for all on connections.

Even though a coastal community may be isolated, it is still linked, along the water line, to other places. Indeed, it is linked to all other coastal communities. Whereas one needs a road in good repair to travel on land, a seaworthy boat joins one coast to others around the world. Water is the great connector. The waves on some Pacific beach may have their origins near Japan. The spent current of a river can be traced to the highest and furthest removed regions of the continental interior.

Today, environmental problems are becoming increasingly global. We are becoming more aware of the interconnectedness of all things, and perhaps nowhere more so than along the coast. If, for example, one of the most serious problems, the greenhouse effect, develops as predicted, sea levels will rise, flooding out hundreds of millions of people who now live on the coasts around the world.

Whether we wish to be or not, we are all part of the same community, linked by the same long, rich, overwhelmingly complex and fragile line.

*At dawn, a sportfishing boat heads out
to sea off Key Biscayne, Florida.*

*Brant Point Lighthouse appears as a
lone sentinel along a stretch of beach in
Nantucket, Massachusetts.*

South Padre Island, Texas. The sun setting on coastal waters frames a sailboat.

Windsurfers off Key West, Florida, glide across an ocean made silver against the afternoon sun.

The landscape of Prince Edward Island, seen here from the air, is famous for its green fields, red soil and sandy beaches.

A lighthouse and the remains of gun emplacements from the Second World War guard the entrance to the harbor of St. John's, Newfoundland.

*Nantucket, Massachusetts. Lush fields
and clapboard farmhouses give this
setting a bucolic appearance.*

An aerial view of Camden Harbor in Camden, Maine.

*Nags Head, North Carolina. Treacherous
shoals and stormy weather off the coast
of North Carolina can complicate
navigation for trading vessels.*

Wealthy estates grace the shoreline of Long Island, New York.

*Mount Baker rises majestically behind
the flickering lights of Vancouver Inner
Harbour, British Columbia.*

San Diego, California. Sailboats and palm trees complement the structures of the city's skyline.

A schooner glides past the Statue of Liberty in New York City Harbor.

The Golden Gate Bridge frames the San Francisco skyline as dawn breaks a fiery red.

Charleston area, South Carolina. Two fishermen hoist a net, heavy with fish, out of water.

*Haida longhouse poles are ghostly
sentinels in the lush vegetation of the
Queen Charlotte Islands, British
Columbia.*

Atlantic City, New Jersey. Sprawled along a barrier beach, Atlantic City boasts new casinos and a vintage boardwalk.

An abandoned coast guard station is surrounded by sand in Carolla, North Carolina.

Fishing weirs, Grand Manan Island,
New Brunswick. Shore-bound herring
are directed into these traps, from which
they will later be netted and hauled
aboard the boats.

Morning view from Cadillac Mountain, Acadia National Park, Maine. A ferry out of Bar Harbor crosses Frenchman Bay on its long journey to Nova Scotia.

Clouds hug the highrises of Seattle, Washington.

*Sunset over Boston, Massachusetts.
Water and sky shimmer with light.*

Fishing boats move out of mist near Rockland, Maine.

The Los Angeles skyline rises out of a sultry, sunny morning.

A sandbar along Oahu's windward shore offers a convenient mooring for Hawaiian boaters.

A view of Annapolis, Maryland. The fishing craft in the bay will later harvest oysters.

PHOTOGRAPH CREDITS